SIN IS LIKE POOP!

SIN IS LIKE POOP!

A MOTHER'S GUIDE TO A MESSY SUBJECT

ESTHER EDWARDS

Copyright © 2015 by Esther Edwards

All rights reserved. No part of this book may be used or reproduced in any manner, stored in a retrieval system, or transmitted in any form or by any means – electronic, mechanical, photocopy, recording, scanning or any other – except in the case of brief quotations in printed reviews, without the prior written permission from the Author.

Unless otherwise indicated, all Scripture quotations are taken from – **THE HOLY BIBLE, NEW INTERNATIONAL VERSION®, NIV® Copyright © 1973, 1978, 1984, 2011 by Biblica, Inc.® Used by permission. All rights reserved worldwide.**

Drawbaugh Publishing Group
444 Allen Drive
Chambersburg, PA 17202

Paperback ISBN 978-1-941746-20-2

eBook ISBN 978-1-941746-21-9

Contents

Foreword vii

CHAPTER 1 – *Sin is like Poop* 1

CHAPTER 2 – *Who Poops?* 9

CHAPTER 3 – *Poop Stinks* 19

CHAPTER 4 – *Poop is Embarrassing* 27

CHAPTER 5 – *Poop is a Mess* 37

CHAPTER 6 – *Sin is like Fertilizer* 45

CHAPTER 7 – *Sin is like Constipation* 53

CHAPTER 8 – *If We Saw Sin as Poop* 62

CHAPTER 9 – *Poop Affects Others* 69

CHAPTER 10 – *Where Does Poop Go?*   *77*

CHAPTER 11 – *Poop is Alienating*   *91*

CHAPTER 12 – *Poop Removal*   *101*

Epilogue   *111*

Foreword

Thank you for picking up my book today! I know it must've been a book you never thought you'd see as a title, so I double-thank you for giving this content matter a try. In a way, this book is my story, my testimony, for I have seen the mess sin causes in my life and in others' lives first hand.

I am an Army wife, homemaker, piano teacher, Bible student, and mother of four. I have lived in Illinois, Virginia, Georgia, South Carolina, and now currently reside in Hawaii. We've been through two deployments, several training separations, and many moves.

My hope in your reading of this devotional is that you will see sin in a new light, but more importantly, see what God can do when we humbly come to Him. May this begin a lot of blessed discussion and lead ultimately to healing and spiritual growth.

Esther

Chapter 1

Sin is like Poop

"For out of the heart come evil thoughts—
murder, adultery, sexual immorality, theft,
false testimony, slander."
Matthew 15:19

As a mother, I have contemplated many deep issues while changing the diapers of my four children. The disgusting waste they emit from their bodies bears an uncanny resemblance to sin in our lives. As I struggle to hold their legs with one hand and clean up their bottoms with the other, they sometimes kick and jerk their bodies against my will, making this process all the more difficult. Frustrated, I hold on tighter, yet they kick even harder. Don't they realize that I am trying to get the smelly, bacteria-filled, health hazard away from them? Don't they understand that if they touch it, it could make them very sick? Don't they know that if they put their dirty hand in their mouth, we'll be bound for the hospital? Gross. Disgusting. Revolting!!

Of course, as babies, they have no concept what in the world poop is. They are blissfully unaware of the bacterial dangers of poop, not to mention the heinous rashes it can cause! To them it's a fabulous new-textured play dough or a toy that goes "splash" in the toilet! To them, it's simply another discovery to be made or another mystery to unfold. (Personally, I'd rather they *not* unfold those dirty diapers!)

Then I put myself in God's shoes for a moment: No matter how many times He cleanses us from sin, we'll sin again and again. We often try to kick God out of the way as we continue to enjoy sinning. Sin entices us, but we are ignorant of the fact that sin is like poop! Yes, God, like our earthly mom, recognizes that sin, like poop, is harmful—and ultimately— eternally fatal for us. We, as little children, do not understand how heinous, unhealthy, and destructive sin truly is. God wants to separate our sins from us, but we keep producing, playing with, and sitting in sin. If we allow Him, He will continually cleanse us.

Are we walking around with sinfully soiled diapers right now? Have we knelt humbly before Him today asking forgiveness and cleansing? Do we ever stop pooping? Do we ever stop sinning? It's a daily need to get rid of the bodily waste just as it is a daily need for us to regularly rid our hearts of the sinful waste within.

PRAYER

It's so true, Holy Father, that my sin is like poop to you. I come to you in my dirty diaper, unclean and unfit to be in your Presence. As my loving Heavenly Father, You readily and gently cleanse me of my disgusting sins just as my earthly mother so lovingly changed my earthly diapers. Yet help me to be willing; willing to allow You to work through the power of the cross in my life. Like a toddler who defiantly and willfully resists his mother as she tries to clean up the poop, I sometimes keep You from doing your job. The results: I will sit in my sin, until I finally allow You to clean my sinful soul. By this time, I have acquired a nasty rash from sitting in my sinfulness.

How do *I* defy You, Lord when I stubbornly refuse to confess my sins of un-forgiveness, laziness, pride, prayerlessness, greed, selfishness, covetousness, _____ (fill in your own blank). Why do I resist You when I know You have what's best for me in mind? Father God, help me to be *willing* and break down the stubbornness in my life. Open my eyes to the damaging sins in my life that I ignore or don't realize are there. Renew my relationship with You and with others. Melt my stubbornness so You can clean me and change me into a clean, usable servant. Amen.

POINTS TO PONDER

As humans, we've all witnessed as others stubbornly resist God's plans to remove sinfulness from their lives. Many times the person we're witnessing is us—we kick, wail, and throw a tantrum as we resist God.

1. *Think of a time you resisted God's desire to change a sinful attitude, thought, or action from your life.*

2. *What kind of "rash" or consequences did you notice?*

3. *How did this distance you from the Lord?*

Scripture to Read: Isaiah 48:4

"For I knew how stubborn you were; your neck muscles were iron, your forehead was bronze."

Scripture to Read: Psalm 78:8

They would not be like their ancestors— a stubborn and rebellious generation, whose hearts were not loyal to God, whose spirits were not faithful to him.

4. **Thinking of the willful child in the poopy diaper and these Scripture references, make a list of attitudes that can accompany resistance.**

5. *What thoughts commonly pervade your thinking when you are resistant to change?*

6. *Using your attitude list from question #4, create another list of the opposites of these attitudes.*

Scripture to Read: Isaiah 1:19-20

19 If you are willing and obedient, you will eat the good things of the land; 20 but if you resist and rebel, you will be devoured by the sword." For the mouth of the Lord has spoken.

Scripture to Read: Psalm 51:12-15

12 Restore to me the joy of your salvation and grant me a willing spirit, to sustain me. 13 Then I will teach transgressors your ways, so that sinners will turn back to you. 14 Deliver me from the guilt of bloodshed, O God, you who are God my Savior, and my tongue will sing of your righteousness. 15 Open my lips, Lord, and my mouth will declare your praise.

7. *Looking at Isaiah 1:19-20 and Psalm 51:12-15, what are the promises received as a result of willing and obedient attitudes?*

8. *How can you (or your group) pray for the openness to abandon the resistant attitudes and embrace the willing ones?*

9. *If you have never known the "joy of salvation," pray for the Lord to wash away your sins with Jesus' blood and to deliver you from guilt. Thank God in your prayer for rescuing you from the guilt of sin and its eternal consequences.*

Chapter 2

Who Poops?

"For all have sinned and fall short of the glory of God." Romans 3:23

The title question "who poops" seems almost rhetorical, but it certainly bears mentioning. The fact that everyone poops is an inarguable point. Every day at some point we must take care of this unpleasant business. Some people have a specific time of day, in the morning perhaps, that they take care of this. Their body has gotten accustomed to that time of day. Some maybe go every other day, but the point is that everyone has to do this.

Everyone poops, but nobody brags about it, especially not at the dinner table! Everyone knows that everyone does it, but we don't typically want to have detailed conversations about how we're pooping lately, unless you have issues that you must discuss with your doctor. Even then, most doctors try to use terms like BM (bowel movement), stool, or fecal matter to make it sound more scientific.

We even go to great lengths to cover over the evidence of what we just had to do. We use liquid drops to minimize the odors, or air fresheners to make the room smell nicer after it's been marred with poop. We turn on the exhaust fan or crack the window open to air out the stench that has polluted the air. We do this especially if we have the unfortunate emergency of needing to go "number 2" at someone else's house.

We were at a family party recently and our cousin's five-year-old son had to go "real bad." The poor little guy cried, "Mom, I don't want to go here, I want to go at HOME." We're not comfortable having to do our "doody" anywhere but the comfort of home if we can manage it. However, you never know when nature will call!

We not only cover over the odors and try to air out the bathroom, but we certainly do not want to admit it was us if there is a clog or toilet overflow! Sure, in your immediate family it's not hard to admit, but if you're at your place of employment or a friend's house: talk about embarrassing! A friend of mine had a problem like that at work, where she had to contact the building janitor to fix the toilet full of humiliation. She was absolutely mortified to have to admit that she was the cause of that.

We want to portray a good image of ourselves: "I'm clean, cool, confident." We want to walk around "like our poop don't stink." Me? Produce something like *that*? Never! I'm way above that! I'm not at *that* level! Yet the inarguable fact is that all of us poop; it's 100% fact, as much as we'd like to avoid it.

So, we've established the well-known fact that everyone poops and can accept it; but, what everyone *doesn't* accept so easily is that everyone sins. Everyone sins, but nobody brags about it. This concept sounds similar to "nobody's perfect," but when it comes down to admitting to it personally, we start to squirm and point fingers in other directions. It is so easy to rationalize our own sins away as being "ok" or "not that bad" while deflecting the focus to *other* people's worse sins. "That guy, he's in prison for murder, he's a big sinner" or "Would you look at her promiscuous lifestyle; wow, God could never forgive her." Jesus says, "You hypocrite, first take the plank out of your own eye, and then you will see clearly to remove the speck from your brother's eye." (Matthew 7:5)

Is my poop better than your poop? It's all utterly detestable, and completely unacceptable. The same can be related to sin: sin is sin and any amount is intolerable to a Holy God. My sin is no better than yours and we can't cover over it with beautiful perfume or a brand new house or an expensive academic degree; not even good deeds cover them.

My kids love when I make fresh chocolate chip cookies at home. They love the taste, the smell, and the yummy gooey texture. But, what if, as I were offering those delicious cookies to them, I also told them that just a quarter ounce of cat poop got mixed into the batter, do you think they would accept them? I mean, I am talking about an amount so small that a doctor would ok it because there was no possible way it could cause any health issue or that you would even taste it. Would YOU try one of these cookies? No one would! That is because even the thought of something so detestable being near us (much less eating it) is despicable to us. Just like the smallest sliver of poop is disgusting to us, the smallest sliver of sin is disgusting to our Almighty Perfect God.

Did you ever take a pen home from work? Have you ever made up an excuse to get out of a dinner date? Both are the smallest of harmless acts, but are disgusting SINS to God. Just as everyone poops, everyone in the history of the world (except One Person) has committed some sin against God. "All of us have become like one who is unclean, and all our righteous acts are like filthy rags…" (Isaiah 64:6).

Psalm 53:3 states that "*everyone* has turned away, *all* have become corrupt; there is no one who does good, *not even one*." There is only one who has not turned away, become corrupt, and who does good: Jesus Christ, the Son of God. Jesus said, "For I have not come to call the righteous, but sinners" (Matthew 9:13). "Sinners" includes everyone, because none of us are righteous. Although our sin is so vile and our efforts are inadequate to cover it, Christ's selfless sacrifice of his very life is sufficient to cover our lowest, cruelest, and most despicable sin.

Admitting the foulness of our deeds puts us on the path to recovery. "If we claim to be without sin, we deceive ourselves and the truth is not in us." (1 John 1:8) God can forgive our sins if we are willing to confess and admit that we are sinners and have faith in Christ's covering over our sinfulness. The Greek word for confess is *homologeo*, meaning "to assent, consent, admit, to promise, to confess publicly, acknowledge openly, profess."

Are we willing to look at ourselves in the mirror and openly acknowledge our imperfect thoughts, actions, and attitudes? John 3:16 promises that "God so loved the world that He gave his one and only Son that whoever believes in him, shall not perish but have eternal life." He's come to save us from sin that separates us from a Holy God, so that we might have the blessed hope of eternal life. This is the good news, the message of hope!

PRAYER

Faithful Father, we praise you for making a way for us, even though we are hopeless sinners by nature. Thank you for Christ, the Lamb of God, who takes away the sins of the world. Lord, I recognize that I myself am a sinner, and I humbly ask for your forgiveness. I realize that I cannot make it to Heaven on my own merit. Even the smallest speck of sin is like poop to You; and I, as well as my human brothers and sisters, fall helplessly short of your glory, God. Please cover over my sinfulness with Your perfection, most Holy Lord. Help me to admit my sins to You humbly and regularly. Amen.

POINTS TO PONDER

We have all witnessed situations where someone is trying to hide their sin. It's often quite painful to have to be the one that must admit sin. Oftentimes, it is me that resists admitting I've sinned and as a proud human, I attempt to hide my sin.

1. *What thoughts come to mind about this ineffectual hiding?*

2. *Can you relate to how the Lord must feel when we are slow to admit that we have sinned whether in deed, thought, or attitude?*

3. *How can we get past our pride and have humility in our admission of sin?*

Scripture to Read: James 2:8-11

8 If you really keep the royal law found in Scripture, "Love your neighbor as yourself,"[a] you are doing right. 9 But if you show favoritism, you sin and are convicted by the law as lawbreakers. 10 For whoever keeps the whole law and yet stumbles at just one point is guilty of breaking all of it. 11 For he who said, "You shall not commit adultery,"[b] also said, "You shall not murder."[c] If you do not commit adultery but do commit murder, you have become a lawbreaker.

4. *How many points of the law must you stumble at to be considered guilty of breaking the whole thing?*

5. *How do you respond to the fact that we are guilty lawbreakers?*

Scripture to Read: Romans 6:23

23 For the wages of sin is death, but the gift of God is eternal life in Christ Jesus our Lord.

6. *Look up the definition of a wage.*

7. *What is the definition of a gift?*

8. *Discuss these opposing definitions.*

9. *From this passage, which would you rather deal with: the wages or the gift?*

10. Ask the Lord to make this Scripture clear in meaning to you. Thank him for this gift in prayer.

Chapter 3

Poop Stinks

*"Jesus said, 'Take ye away the stone.'
Martha, the sister of him that was dead,
saith unto him, 'Lord, by this time he
stinketh: for he hath been dead four days.'"*
John 11:39 (KJV)

Congratulations on the understatement of the year! Poop has to be one of the foulest smells to the human nose causing the most wrinkled faces, the fastest nose pinching, and the loudest exclamations of, "EWW!! What's that smell?" Our sense of smell sends quick messages to our brain and if poop is involved, the message is, "Get out of here!" "Change that diaper!" or "Clean up the cat litter!"

Smell is also known as the most nostalgic of all our senses. Because of the way the olfactory nerve travels from the front of the face, straight through to your brain, it passes through the midbrain, the center for emotion and memory. That's why smells, good and bad, are so linked to our emotions and memories. Smell has the power to delight or disgust us. When I smell the fresh aroma of eucalyptus leaves, I am instantly taken back to my grandmother's fragrant home in Upper Peninsula Michigan. I'm drawn back to a cozy, homey place where love abounds.

Imagine for yourself the most pleasant aroma that transports you to memories of comfort and love. Warm chocolate chip cookies? A tender roast beef? Fresh-baked cinnamon rolls? Whatever it is, imagine that scent and take a trip down memory lane.

Now flip the coin and imagine the worst, most heinous, rancid poop smell you've ever encountered (the worst vomit, body odor, or garbage smell will do also). For me, even as a mother of four children, I have seen countless poopy diapers. I have even changed the diapers of other children as a babysitter, (which smell worse than the diapers of your own kids). I've seen and smelled diarrhea, yellow poop, brown poop, and green poop, with varying degrees of foulness.

However, the hands-down worst smell I have ever smelled I experienced while we were stationed at Fort Stewart, Georgia. While perusing the canned food aisle at Wal-Mart with my toddler and preschooler, out of nowhere, appeared a horrifyingly foul odor. What WAS that? I examined my two children to see if I had a diaper to change, but they were innocent. As I continued to push my cart, the smell only grew stronger. As I turned the corner, I discovered the appallingly offensive culprit: a confused and unaware elderly gentleman, strolling the aisles with an explosive diarrheal accident covering his gray sweatpants!

What to do? How can I help? Sir, can I buy you some new pants? Didn't he recognize the horrendous mess in his pants causing his fellow shoppers to cover their noses and run for the air freshener aisle? Do I call store management? What could *they* do?

In this awkward predicament, even my four-year-old daughter blurted out, rather loudly, "EEWWW! Mommy, what's that smell?"

"SHHH! It's none of our business!" I whisper-yelled, trying to squelch her questions. The best thing I could do was to cover my nose, get the essentials faster than a cheetah, and abandon ship! As we made our escape, the gasps from other shoppers proved the unstoppable stench was a force to be reckoned with.

Just as the unfortunate gray sweat pants stunk horribly, so does our sin offend the nostrils of our Holy God. When we are unaware of our sinful bitterness, unwilling attitude, worry, or pride, perhaps we cannot sense it unless the Holy Spirit makes us aware of it. However, our Holy God can certainly detect any hint of sin with his spiritual "sense of smell." How often does He need to pinch his nose in disgust at our foul messes? As Ecclesiastes 10:1 says, "As dead flies give perfume a bad smell, so a little folly outweighs wisdom and honor." Our folly and sin will always outweigh what little wisdom and honor we possess.

Other times, we are certainly aware of our imperfections and realize our need to confess to the Lord, and even to others. As 1 John 1:9 promises, "If we confess our sins, he is faithful and just to forgive us our sins and to cleanse us from all unrighteousness." What an amazing promise to be welcomed into the Lord's love for cleansing from our sinful, smelly messes that we can't even begin to fix ourselves. Through the Lord's faithfulness, we are made white as snow.

In the Old Testament, priests would offer "fragrant offerings" on the altar to God—whether they were grain offerings or lamb offerings—they were "pleasing to God." These sacrifices sound good to me too! Mmmm…. cornbread and rack of lamb roasting! These offerings were accompanied with praise, confession of sins, and gratitude. Some offerings were guilt offerings necessary to cover sin.

In Ephesians 5:2, we see that, "Christ loved us and gave himself up for us as a fragrant offering and sacrifice to God." The sweetest smelling sacrifice of all was that of God's precious Son pouring out His life for the sins of the world. God iterates how He feels at Christ's baptism in Luke 3:22b: "You are my Son, whom I love; with you I am well pleased." How pleasing this aroma is to the Father, as opposed to our inadequate efforts to cover over our putrid sinfulness.

Even if the elderly gentleman had used the finest, most costly cologne to cover over his poopy pants, it would've been inadequate. Christ's pleasing sacrifice is essential to bring true cleansing to our foul-smelling hearts. When we accept that Christ's sacrifice is our only hope, our lives can be righteous and fragrant to our Holy God too. When we are in Christ, the stench of sin is covered and the fragrance of Christ reigns!

PRAYER

Most Holy Father, I confess to you my displeasing state as a sinner. I know You must hold Your nose when I am bitter toward others, prideful, anxious, and spiteful. Father, please forgive me for these sins that flow from my heart on a daily basis. I ask you to clean me and make me pure, make my life as a pure white lily, pleasing to Your senses and lovely in Your eyes. Father, make me aware of the sins I don't realize and bring me to a place of knowledge and wisdom. I thank you for the incredible sacrifice of Jesus Christ, the most pleasing aroma of all, my blessed Savior who gave his life fully and willingly, to rescue a wretch such as I. Oh God, thank You for this indescribable gift! Amen.

POINTS TO PONDER

We've all gotten a "whiff" of some unpleasant attitudes and even words. Unfortunately, oftentimes these attitudes and words come from our own sinful hearts.

1. *Make a list of the current rotten-smelling sinful attitudes you're aware of in yourself. (i.e. envy, strife, quarreling, rage, greed, bitterness, ingratitude, complaining, idolatry, deceit, to name a few.)*

2. *Imagine that the Lord can "smell" these sinful attitudes; what do these attitudes smell like to Him? (i.e. rotten fish, a dump truck, dirty gym clothes, etc.)*

Scripture to Read: Psalm 141:2

2 May my prayer be set before you like incense; may the lifting up of my hands be like the evening sacrifice.

Scripture to Read: Revelation 8:3-4.

3 Another angel, who had a golden censer, came and stood at the altar. He was given much incense to offer, with the prayers of all God's people, on *the golden altar in front of the throne. **4** The smoke of the incense, together with the prayers of God's people, went up before God from the angel's hand.*

3. *In contrast to what displeases God, what can we give that has a pleasing aroma to God?*

4. *To contrast the list in #2, make a new list of pleasing prayers and praises as opposites of each sinful attitude. Offer up these sweet prayers to the Lord, asking him to have Jesus rule over each sinful attitude.*

Chapter 4

Poop is Embarrassing

"Instead of your shame you will receive a double portion, and instead of disgrace you will rejoice in your inheritance. And so you will inherit a double portion in your land, and everlasting joy will be yours."
Isaiah 61:7

Why does this embarrass us so much when everyone does it? Why do we close doors and have "alone time" in the restroom? Why do kids in diapers slink off into a corner to do their business? Undoubtedly, these are not our proudest moments, but everyday we have to deal with it. We don't proclaim to the world, "I just pooped!" That is, unless a child has successfully completed potty training or a rejoicing hospital patient is now regularly pooping indicating they are functioning well! By and large, though, the general population doesn't share these moments publicly.

It's really no wonder we want to hide behind a door, in the comfort of our own home, when we have to poop. Images involved in the process are: grunting, red-face, sweating, and foul odor. No wonder we bring reading material into the bathroom; not only does it pass the time, but it's a distraction from all this unpleasantness! It's also interesting how many products are available to hide the odors of poop and the sounds. Some eastern cultures have musical toilets in public restrooms to cover the unpleasant sounds associated with pooping. You can press a button and a toilet-flushing sound or musical ditty plays so you can cover over embarrassing poop sounds.

I remember a time when my sisters and I all shared a hotel room in Hawaii for a family reunion we attended. Most of us were in high school and college—prime time for extra embarrassment! One sister had clogged the hotel room toilet. Unfortunately, we were helpless to fix the toilet on our own. We forced her to call the front desk for assistance. When the plumber came to the door we made her answer the door, while the rest of us hid in the bedroom, leaving her all alone to face the shame.

Just as poop is certainly not an event we trumpet from the treetops, our sinfulness is embarrassing and shameful…especially when caught. Think back to the original sin in the Garden of Eden: Adam, Eve, and the forbidden fruit. After the serpent convinced them and they partook of the forbidden fruit, out of shame and embarrassment, they hid. Adam confessed, "I heard you in the garden, and I was afraid because I was naked, so I hid." (Genesis 3:11) They felt ashamed of their nakedness and disobedience, and probably had the guilt of fruit juice all over their faces too. So like guilty children with poopy diapers, they hid in the bushes and tried to cover their shameful nakedness with leaves.

Sin had created an instant barrier between God and his children. In a perfect world, we want to live righteously and share all aspects of our lives with the Lord. The ugly truth is that this side of Heaven, sin will always be present in our lives. Just as we are embarrassed about poop, we are ashamed of our sins and attempt to hide them from our omniscient God. As humans, we carry the burden of shame and are helpless to fix the problem of sin. How could I possibly approach my King stained with my reprehensible sins?

Do not forget that the Lord came down and placed Himself in a human body and understands us intimately. He walked in our shoes as a human, experiencing all the temptations, emotions, difficulties, and trials we live with daily. Jesus is familiar with all sins from little white lies to murderous hatred; from impure thoughts to adulterous unfaithfulness. He sees them because He carried every single one on His shoulders as He gave up His very life to conquer them with His all-powerful sacrifice.

So what? So let us approach the throne of grace with our giant bag of dirty diapers. Jesus' love for us is capable and sufficient to cleanse even the dirtiest and poopiest of diapers that we could create. Christ's amazing act on the cross redeems us from our sins, cleansing us. "In him we have redemption through his blood, the forgiveness of sins, in accordance with the riches of God's grace that he lavished on us" (Ephesians 1:7-8a).

Christ can wipe away our shame and guilt if we come humbly and reverently to the mercy seat, where He serves mercy daily for anyone who comes to partake. It is free. There is an unending supply, so bring all your sins and trade them for forgiveness and abundant life! "I have swept away your offenses like a cloud, your sins like the morning mist. Return to me, for I have redeemed you" (Isaiah 44:22-23).

PRAYER

Father, give us clean hands and pure hearts. May we come to You, in our deep need, to wash in the bounteous blood of Christ. To drink of the unending living water that quenches our spiritual thirstiness forever. To eat of the Bread of Life: Jesus, the sustainer of life. If this is the trade off, I'm in: to unashamedly, leave all my sins and exchange it for forgiveness and mercy! Holy Spirit, remind me daily of this gift I possess and remind me to leave my shameful sins at Your feet and to remain steadfast in Your forgiveness. Help me to be willing to confess my sins and to not be ashamed of my sinfulness, but allow You to see me and change me from the inside out. Amen.

POINTS TO PONDER

We've all certainly witnessed scandals on the news, lies, extra-marital affairs, theft, and the like. How embarrassing for your sins to be broadcast for the world to judge and see! We've all been in equally embarrassing situations we wanted to keep private, especially when they involve our own sins.

1. *How do you feel in a situation where your sins are exposed?*

2. *Mark or circle words or phrases that resonate with you as you read the following Scripture.*

Scripture to Read: Psalm 139.

1 You have searched me, Lord, and you know me. 2 You know when I sit and when I rise; you perceive my thoughts from afar. 3 You discern my going out and my lying down; you are familiar with all my ways. 4 Before a word is on my tongue you, Lord, know it completely. 5 You hem me in behind and before, and you lay your hand upon me. 6 Such knowledge is too wonderful for me, too lofty for me to attain. 7 Where can I go from your Spirit? Where can I flee from your presence? 8 If I go up to the heavens, you are there; if I make my bed in the depths, you are there. 9 If I rise on the wings of the dawn, if I settle on the far side of the sea, 10 even there your hand will *guide me, your right hand will hold me fast.* **11** *If I say, "Surely the darkness will hide me and the light become night around me," ***12*** *even the darkness will not be dark to you; the night will shine like the day, for darkness is as light to you.* **13** *For you created my inmost being; you knit me together in my mother's womb.* **14** *I praise you because I am fearfully and wonderfully made; your works are wonderful, I know that full well.* **15** *My frame was not hidden from you when I was made in the secret place, when I was woven together in the depths of the earth.* **16** *Your eyes saw my unformed body; all the days ordained for me were written in your book before one of them came to be.* **17** *How precious to me are your thoughts, God! How vast is the sum of them!* **18** *Were I to count them, they would outnumber the grains of sand—when I awake, I am still with you.* **19** *If only you, God, would slay the wicked! Away from me, you who are bloodthirsty!* **20** *They speak of you with evil intent; your adversaries misuse your name.* **21** *Do I not hate those who hate you, Lord, and abhor those who are in rebellion against you?* **22** *I have nothing but hatred for them; I count them my enemies.* **23** *Search me, God, and know my heart; test me and know my anxious thoughts. 24 See if there is any offensive way in me, and lead me in the way everlasting.*

3. *In our most private places, who is always there through everything?*

4. *Circle the places in this passage that the psalmist could have tried to hide from the Lord. Write all the hiding places below.*

5. *Where can he go from His presence?*

6. *How or where do you try to hide from the Lord?*

7. *Looking at verses 23-24, what conclusions must we come to regarding our private sins?*

8. *What areas of your life do you attempt to hide or keep from the Lord? (i.e. relationships, habits, attitudes, emotions, desires, etc.)*

9. *How may your group (or you) pray regarding these areas?*

Chapter 5

Poop is a Mess

"Depart, depart, go out from there! Touch no unclean thing! Come out from it and be pure…" Isaiah 52:11

My father-in-law tells a story about a time when he walked into his one-year-old son's bedroom and was blown away by the stench of a gargantuan poopy mess! The sight he saw was a baby covered in excrement. The wee one had smeared poop on the walls, in the crib, and in his hair! When dear father had regained his composure he did what any good dad would do— he went to his wife and said, "He wants *you!*"

I'm sure you can think of a time you were knocked over by an overpowering stench and the sight of poop (or trash, or vomit) strewn all about.

It makes you ask yourself, "Where do I begin with this?" How about rubber gloves, clothespins, and a HAZMAT suit, for starters?

Think about how the Lord must feel when we have made a humongous mess of things and we come to him, covered in sin and all the consequences. Cleaning up this mess will not be pleasant, yet completely necessary. As a mother will gingerly remove the soiled clothing from her child, then the diaper, does not God gently remove us from our messes, one step at a time? It will not be pleasant, but necessary for us to be able to continue on.

Take the story of Joseph, for example. Many messes resulted from his father's favoritism and his brothers' hatred of him. Joseph's brothers sold him into slavery. They also lied to their father saying that a wild animal killed Joseph. Sin upon sin leads to many consequences not just for Joseph, but for the other family members too. Guilt eats away at his brothers and grief strikes his father deeply. Joseph's story is one of blessed redemption where God uses all of these circumstances to gradually bring healing to this family and salvation to the nation of Israel. Joseph's family had a mangled mess of sin that had a ripple-effect of consequences, just like the one-year-old's poop explosion. Yet, one situation at a time, God forgives each sin and cleanses this family so they can be together again. To read it in its entirety, check out Genesis chapters 37 and 39-50. It's long, but worth it and one of my favorite Bible stories.

As God step-by-step brought cleansing and healing to Joseph's family, similarly does a mother clean her child covered in excrement. After she has extracted her baby from the poopy clothes, his mother will put him in the tub and begin to wash the poop from his dirty body. Later, she'll have to clean and disinfect the walls, the bed, rugs, floors, and the clothes. Doesn't the Lord have to do the same when our sin explodes all over our lives and into the lives of others?

Although the mother may be initially shocked, she rolls up her sleeves, and cleans her child. In contrast, our sins never shock our Heavenly Father; for Him, there is nothing new under the sun. It's interesting to me that my children will be absolutely disgusted even by dirty dishes and try to wash them without touching them. As a mom, I cannot relate for I have seen too many poopy, barf-y, booger-y, bloody messes to even flinch at a dirty dish. Our omniscient Lord has seen a wide array of sins; thus, whatever we bring to Him, He will not be surprised. Think of the sins He witnessed while on earth: betrayal, lies, deceit, plots of murder, adultery, anger—the entire spectrum of sin. Why is it our instinct to hide from the Lord? When He sees us in our sinful messes, He is neither shocked nor surprised. He knows exactly what to do and can clean us and justify us.

This justification comes only through our Lord and Savior Jesus Christ. His deep love for us caused him to endure the cross for our sake. We are absolutely helpless to rid ourselves of sin without the blood of Jesus Christ. Hebrews 9:22 says that "…the law requires that nearly everything be cleansed with blood, and without the shedding of blood there is no forgiveness." In Romans 4:25 we see that it was Jesus that "was delivered over to death for our sins and raised to life for our justification." Our sins died with Christ, and we are raised with him to eternal life just as He was resurrected from the dead. When we put our faith in Christ's work on the cross for our sins, we are justified, "just as if I had never sinned."

PRAYER

Lord Jesus, do my sins shock you? Do they ever surprise you? I know that you see all things before they even happen. "Before a word is on my tongue you, Lord, know it completely." (Psalm 139:4). You know that I am unworthy, sinful and will make mistakes as long as I am human and live on this fallen earth. Father, help me to realize that coming to you should be my first move when I have dirty sins in my life. Even though my sins would shock others around me, You are not shocked, but pleased when I come to you to be cleaned and made whole again.

Lord, what messes I've made in my life: sins that have had reverberating consequences not just for me but also my loved ones. Yet somehow, when I came back to you and left the sin, confessed my shortcomings to You, You welcomed me back with open arms. You have not only cleansed me, you've used these times of trial to grow me spiritually. May I get over the things that inhibit me from confession and humbly and willingly kneel in your presence as you forgive and make me into a clean vessel, fit for your Holy Spirit. May I not forget what You did on the cross for me and depend on Your perfect sacrifice for my salvation from hell, eternal separation from You, Lord. Amen.

POINTS TO PONDER

We have all been in the situation where our sin has caused a mess, whether it's minor or major. Unfortunately, we find ourselves looking at the mess and unsure what direction to take to begin performing clean-up.

1. *What sinful mess have you made, (present or past) that the Lord needs to or has already conducted clean up on?*

2. *What thoughts or feelings come as you attempt to decide how to begin?*

3. *How will you seek the Lord in order to be cleaned and forgiven?*

Scripture to Read: John 8:2-11

2 *At dawn he appeared again in the temple courts, where all the people gathered around him, and he sat down to teach them.* **3** *The teachers of the law and the Pharisees brought in a woman caught in adultery. They made her stand before the group* **4** *and said to Jesus, "Teacher, this woman was caught in the act of adultery.* **5** *In the Law Moses commanded us to stone such women. Now what do you say?"* **6** *They were using this question as a trap, in order to have a basis for accusing him. But Jesus bent down and started to write on the ground with his finger.* **7** *When they kept on questioning him, he straightened up and said to them, "Let any one of you who is without sin be the first to throw a stone at her."* **8** *Again he stooped down and wrote on the ground.*

9 *At this, those who heard began to go away one at a time, the older ones first, until only Jesus was left, with the woman still standing there.* **10** *Jesus straightened up and asked her, "Woman, where are they? Has no one condemned you?"* **11** *"No one, sir," she said. "Then neither do I condemn you," Jesus declared. "Go now and leave your life of sin."*

4. *How does Jesus approach the woman caught in adultery?*

5. *What a mess they brought Jesus into, but how does Jesus react to their accusations of the woman?*

6. *As Christ has forgiven you, in what situations can you extend His loving-kindness and forgiveness to others?*

7. *Praise the Lord for His amazing grace and ask Him to forgive whatever current sins you have. Ask him to help you extend this forgiveness to others.*

CHAPTER 6

Sin Is like Fertilizer

*"You intended to harm me, but God
intended it for good to accomplish what is
now being done, the saving of many lives."
Genesis 50:20*

As disgusting and unwanted as poop can be, there is a demographic who uses it in their profession: farmers and agriculturists. Poop, full of NPK: nitrogen-phosphorus-potassium, is rich in nutrients for plants. The best organic fertilizer, according to tropicalpermaculture.com, is "chicken poo or blood and bone meal or fish extract…[which] contains the NPK in varying ratios." Gardeners say compost is "black gold." In 1908, a contractor paid the city of Shanghai $31,000 in gold for the "privilege" of collecting 78,000 tons of human waste and carting it off to spread on fields. My uncle who is an avid gardener participates in a program called "Zoo-Doo," where he loads up his truck with animal manure from the local zoo for his garden. Who knew poop could be desirable for anything?

My dad grew up on a cattle farm in northern Michigan and in the winter, the animals slept inside the barn. The cows would indiscriminately poop anywhere, so the poop really starts to build up — about three to four feet high! He would have to put straw down over the manure and in the springtime, all that manure would get cleaned out of the barn. Then he would shovel it into a manure spreader, which hooks up to a tractor. The farmers will then spray it over the fields, spreading it out in healthy doses. The nitrates in the manure would help to feed clover and alfalfa, but it must be spread out evenly or else it would "burn" the crops if they are too concentrated.

Think about all the behind-the-scenes stuff that happens on farms next time you have a glass of milk! It's bizarre to think that the smelly piles of waste could have a good purpose that can help create healthy plants and vegetables. Of course, there's a process the waste must go through involving heat over time to kill any bacteria that's present, *then* the material is usable and helpful. It must be processed and rendered safe before it's a usable product.

So if there are ways to use poop to nourish plants and gardens, the Master Gardener, our Lord, likewise finds ways to use our sins. Take Jacob, the deceiver, as an example. He lied and tricked his father into giving him the first-born blessing, had to flee his angry brother, wrestled with God, and finally God made him into Israel, the father of his people. However, just as with fertilizer, the sin must be processed before it's usable. Sin must go through God's process of forgiveness before it's used to fertilize our lives and help us to grow. "The Lord disciplines the one he loves, and he chastens everyone he accepts as his son…No discipline seems pleasant at the time, but painful. Later on, however, it produces a harvest of righteousness and peace for those who have been trained by it." (Hebrews 12: 6,11). At times we are disciplined for our sins and this is part of the growth we experience.

The most powerful part of my testimony demonstrates the Lord using what Satan, the enemy, intended for evil as God masterfully changed it into something good. As a pastor's daughter, I fell into temptation and sin, resulting in me becoming an unmarried pregnant young woman. Initially, my heart was full of shame and regret, but God used this experience to change my judgmental attitudes into blossoming compassion for fellow sinners. What a messy pile of poop my sin was, yet when I repented, God took it, forgave me, and used it to fertilize my heart. He transformed my shameful and ugly Pharisee-heart into a humble compassionate heart. Only the work of a Master Gardener could accomplish such feats. Hallelujah, for Satan intended it for evil, but God intended it for good (Genesis 50:20).

Poop cannot be useful as fertilizer unless it's put in a proper place and at the proper time. Does not our all-knowing Lord, know this as He recycles sin, processes it, and uses it as fertilizer in proper amounts for redemptive works in our hearts? I am encouraged that trials I go through are not in vain, but have purpose in time. He has been faithful in the past, He will continue to be faithful in the future by disciplining me, forgiving me for my sins, and growing compassion in me.

PRAYER

Wise Gardener and Blessed Father, I thank you that You have the power to transform sin into something that helps to grow Your goodness in me. You have forgiven me and powerfully used my sins as catalysts for change. Despite the mess of sin, Your forgiveness through the cross of Christ purifies us and makes us clean. We inherit YOUR compassion and righteousness, becoming able servants of your kingdom. Thank You for the example of Jacob and how his sins are part of his story and how You changed him from a deceiver to the father of Israel. May we realize the purposes You have for us, even our sins, as we lay our sins at the foot of Your cross; we ask not only for forgiveness, but purpose. Amen.

POINTS TO PONDER

We've all experienced times in life where we've sinned and figure that it's a doomed mess. God sees more than that. He understands that whatever we've done, He can process and use in a way that promotes growth in our hearts.

1. *How can God use sin to "fertilize" our hearts and help them grow?*

2. *Think of a time when God used your sin and through forgiveness, used it to grow a fruit of the Spirit in you. Share with someone or journal about it.*

Scripture to Read: Genesis 50:15-21

15 When Joseph's brothers saw that their father was dead, they said, "What if Joseph holds a grudge against us and pays us back for all the wrongs we did to him?" 16 So they sent word to Joseph, saying, "Your father left these instructions before he died: 17 'This is what you are to say to Joseph: I ask you to forgive your brothers the sins and the wrongs they committed in treating you so badly.' Now please forgive the sins of the servants of the God of your father." When their message came to him, Joseph wept. 18 His brothers then came and threw themselves down before him. "We are your slaves," they said. 19 But Joseph said to them, "Don't be afraid. Am I in the place of God? 20 You intended to harm me, but God intended it for good to accomplish what is now being done, the saving of many lives. 21 So then, don't be afraid. I will provide for you and your children." And he reassured them and spoke kindly to them.

Sin is like Fertilizer

3. *After all the dirty deeds Joseph's brothers had committed against him, how was Joseph able to forgive them?*

4. *How did he view the outcome of his life?*

5. *How did God use sinful situations, attitudes and experiences to fertilize the lives of Joseph and his brothers?*

6. *How has God used the sin in your own life to fertilize your outlook and perspective of things?*

7. *How could He potentially use some present trials?*

8. *Journal or share with the group and praise Him for what He's done in the past and for what He will do in the future!*

Chapter 7

Sin is like Constipation

"Blessed is the one whose transgressions are forgiven, whose sins are covered."
Psalm 32:1

A friend of mine was dealing with chronic and severe back pain. She was in such pain, that the doctor prescribed pain medication. While the medication helped ease the back pain she dealt with, the unfortunate side effect was constipation of the bowels. As a result, she couldn't poop for an entire week! To alleviate the constipation, she had to take a laxative and drink a lot of water in order to move those bowels. Pardon my bluntness, but when she was finally able to poop, because of the build-up, the outcome was very painful, large, and even bloody. Despite the pain, once she was on the other side of the pain and it was all out, she experienced a huge relief and joy for now she could function as a human again!

Similarly, a few years ago my husband had a major surgery after which the doctor prescribed pain medication to cope with the pain. He only took them for a few days because he could not stand the side effect of constipation and would rather deal with the post-surgery pain than with the pain of constipation. Either way he had to deal with pain, but he preferred the surgery pain to the constipation angst.

My point here is that pooping is a necessary natural function in life; if not done with some regularity, it will cause you pain, strife, and the inability to function normally. In a spiritual sense, we also need to open up spiritually to confess and rid ourselves of sins that cause spiritual pain and strife. Isn't it true that we can start to feel the pain of spiritual constipation when things aren't dealt with? Without getting these things out of our systems, bitterness, envy, or whatever kind of spiritual gunk, churns around inside, blocking spiritual progress. Only through the Lord will we receive forgiveness, removal of sins, and the ability to start over.

In Psalm 32:3-4, the psalmist David, describes pain from failing to acknowledge his sin before the Lord:

> *When I kept silent, my bones wasted away through my groaning all day long. For day and night your hand was heavy on me; my strength was sapped as in the heat of summer.*

As we experience pain from physical constipation of the bowels, we can equally feel pain from unconfessed sin. I have experienced this same spiritual pain, holding in big secrets and sins, that I can't handle on my own. Although these things can be painful and difficult to get out, we must or we'll continue to groan and waste away all day long, feeling heavy and weak as David describes in the psalm. Shouldn't we prefer the pain of confession to the pain of holding it in, which offers no relief?

The Psalm goes on to say in verse 5:

> *Then I acknowledged my sin to you and did not cover up my iniquity. I said, "I will confess my transgressions to the Lord." And you forgave the guilt of my sin.*

What a relief we can experience if we come, honestly before the Lord, asking Him for forgiveness. And He so readily forgives the guilt of our sin.

May we experience the blessing of forgiven sins and the lightness of putting down the heavy burdens of our secrets and sins.

PRAYER

Father, I recognize that my sins are just like poop. Without confession of sins, I walk around spiritually constipated, a very ineffective witness of Your light, bogged down by the baggage and burden of my sins. Lord, help me to understand my daily need for confession of sins to You. Convict my heart of those sins that take over my life and consume me. Heavenly Father, help me to let go of my sinful attitudes and embrace compassion for those around me. I don't want to be a Pharisee, but I can resemble one so often. I want to be the woman who anointed your feet with expensive perfume and dried them with her hair. I want to be one who has the capacity to love and forgive because I have also been loved and forgiven. Lord forgive me for not extending the compassion to others that you have extended to me. Mature me in this way: Holy Spirit, remind me of my wrong spirit and may I lay it down at Your cross and pick up Your forgiveness in exchange. Amen.

POINTS TO PONDER

All of us have experienced times of heaviness and burden. Oftentimes we don't recognize that some of the burdens we carry are actually sinful attitudes, emotions, thoughts, or habits. Once we recognize them, we can confess them, be forgiven, and feel light and free!

Scripture to Read: Psalm 32:3-4

3 When I kept silent, my bones wasted away through my groaning all day long. 4 For day and night your hand was heavy on me; my strength was sapped as in the heat of summer.

1. *What kind of spiritual groaning and heaviness have you experienced and why? Share with a prayer partner if possible.*

Scripture to Read: Psalm 51:10-12

10 Create in me a pure heart, O God, and renew a steadfast spirit within me. 11 Do not cast me from your presence or take your Holy Spirit from *me. **12** Restore to me the joy of your salvation and grant me a willing spirit, to sustain me.*

2. Look up the word "pure"; what does it mean to have a pure heart?

3. Look up the meaning of "steadfast" in the dictionary. How can you practice this virtue?

4. Have you ever felt you had been cast from God's presence or devoid of the Holy Spirit? Explain.

5. What sins inhibit the Holy Spirit from freely working in you? Confess these before God.

Sin is like Constipation

6. *Do you know the joy of restoration as described in verse 12? Thank the Lord for it if you have experienced it!*

7. *Pray these verses over yourself, putting your name into the passage.*

   Create in _____ a pure heart, O God, and renew a steadfast spirit within _____. Do not cast _____ from your presence or take your Holy Spirit from _____. Restore unto _____ the joy of your salvation and grant _____ a willing spirit, to sustain _____.

Chapter 8

If We Saw Sin as Poop

"I have swept away your offenses like a cloud, your sins like the morning mist... Sing for joy, you heavens, for the Lord has done this..." Isaiah 44:22-23

One busy morning, my husband and I were quickly preparing to get out the door. I was running around getting some clean clothes for my husband and he was going to hop in the shower. He looked at the clock and then decided that he didn't have time to shower.

"You have 15 minutes, you can get in the shower," I told him.

Firmly, he had decided, "no" I don't have enough time, so he proceeded to brush his teeth and wet down his hair so he could comb it.

He grabbed the nearest towel that he could find to dry his head off. As I tidied up the bathroom of the used towels and dirty clothes, I looked down and saw *it* on the bath rug in the restroom: POOP! Smeared on the rug and on the toilet!

"EWWW!!!" I shrieked.

"What?" he asked.

"There's poop on the floor!"

All the while he was using the towel to dry his hair when it dawned on him that the towel he was using he had picked up near the poop smear. He examined the towel, only to be horrified that this towel was also tainted... with POOP!!

"Is there any on my head?!!"

I quickly examined his head and didn't see any signs of poop in his hair, but on his forehead there was a little brown spot.

"AHHHHH!!"

He began stripping off all his clothes and violently throwing them down on the floor. Apparently now he had time for that shower.

Would he have jumped in the shower if I had not found the speck of poop on his forehead? Probably not. Do we treat sins in our lives with a similar intensity? Rarely. So often, sins are allowed to stay.

If We Saw Sin as Poop

We grow accustomed to their presence, ignoring or forgetting that they are present. Consider the illustration in James 1:23-24: "Anyone who listens to the word but does not do what it says is like someone who looks at his face in a mirror and immediately forgets what he looks like." Can you imagine if my husband hadn't had me examine his face and he had gone out to work with the brown on his forehead? He may have gotten some strange looks! Similarly, we are not fit to be in communion with the Lord with "brown" on our lives. We will also struggle to be in community with others with sins encroaching and causing problems.

We must treat sinfulness with the severity of Matthew 5:29: "If your right eye causes you to stumble, gouge it out and throw it away. It is better for you to lose one part of your body than for your whole body to be thrown into hell." Not to be translated literally, the point is that we ought to get rid of the offending sin and its cause as quickly and completely as we would get rid of poop on our forehead! Whether the sins are our own, or those of our children, we need to eradicate them swiftly! What was my husband's reaction to the poop on his head? Nothing short of full body cleaning; "make sure I shampooed that poop out of my hair FULLY!"

We need to immerse ourselves beneath the fountain of the Lord's perfect sacrifice and lead our children to do the same. Lather up with the bar of the Holy Spirit and pray for forgiveness at the first sign of sinful attitudes, thoughts, or actions. Unchecked, more and more becomes acceptable and our standards decline and diminish over time. It is not merely hearing the Word and so deceiving ourselves, but *doing* what it says (James 1:22). May we continually bring ourselves to the Lamb of God who takes away the sins of the world!

PRAYER

King of kings, we recognize Your holy perfection and our struggle as sinners. Thank you for the provision of Jesus Christ, the Lamb that atones for our sins. May we recognize prideful, selfish, bitter, and angry sin, even a speck of it, as a great offense to You and extremely harmful to our souls. May we learn how to recognize sin for what it is by staying rooted in Your Word, full of knowledge and wisdom. May we also have the wisdom to recognize our need for cleansing from harmful sins. May we continually do battle with sin, within ourselves, our children, and our church. Amen.

POINTS TO PONDER

We can all probably name a few sins that we may have only a "speck" of in our lives. We may grow accustomed to it and dismiss it as unimportant. If we viewed it as the Lord does, we most assuredly would want immediate cleansing.

1. *Do you deal with sins swiftly or do you let them linger?*

2. *Make a list of sins in you and your family that seem to linger, whether they are between siblings, between parent and child, or extended family.*

Scripture to Read: James 1:19-25

***19** My dear brothers and sisters, take note of this: Everyone should be quick to listen, slow to speak and slow to become angry, **20** because human anger does not produce the righteousness that*

God desires. **21** *Therefore, get rid of all moral filth and the evil that is so prevalent and humbly accept the word planted in you, which can save you.* **22** *Do not merely listen to the word, and so deceive yourselves. Do what it says.* **23** *Anyone who listens to the word but does not do what it says is like someone who looks at his face in a mirror* **24** *and, after looking at himself, goes away and immediately forgets what he looks like.* **25** *But whoever looks intently into the perfect law that gives freedom, and continues in it—not forgetting what they have heard, but doing it—they will be blessed in what they do.*

4. *What kinds of sins has God's Word illuminated about you that you weren't aware of?*

5. *Have you experienced this freedom and blessing from applying God's word? Share.*

If We Saw Sin as Poop 67

6. *How can you look intently into the perfect law this week and apply it to receive freedom and the Lord's blessing?*

7. *What "moral filth" (verse 21) permeates your life and how can you practically get rid of it?*

8. *How can God's Word planted in us save us from prevalent evil?*

9. *Ask the Lord to guide you and your family to recognize sin and how to bring it to Him for forgiveness daily.*

Chapter 9

Poop Affects Others

"He committed all the sins his father had done before him..." 1 Kings 15:3

Uncle Manny, as a kid, did not like to use a toilet. He preferred to go outside in nature, amidst the fruit trees they had on their property, to do his business. Sometimes he would forget to bury his poop. So, as his brothers were picking fruit or playing outside, they would accidentally step in his poop! "Why don't you just use the toilet," they complained.

Uncle Manny grew up and had two children. He and his wife were working on building a house with plans to sell it. While he was showing the house-in-progress to a potential buyer, one of his two young children, pooped in one of the upstairs rooms of the house. Using a rock as toilet paper, the child flippantly tossed it down to the first floor and hit the potential buyer in the head! That house showing probably didn't end in a sale. Furious, Uncle Manny disciplined both children severely because neither one would rat the other one out.

If you've ever stepped in dog poop (or been hit in the head with a poopy rock!), you can relate to the frustration with this open-pooping philosophy. It creates quite a mess for your shoes and if you don't realize it soon enough, it can get tracked all over carpets and floors! Soon, there are lots of stinky messes to clean up. Not only that, but his philosophy came back to haunt him when his children adopted his habit and took it to a new level! I can't help but think that the "sins" of the father affected the son, and reflected back on the father too.

In the Bible, King David took Bathsheba and committed adultery with her. She was not his wife, she was Uriah's wife. When she became pregnant, David panicked and sent Uriah to a fierce part of the war, knowing he would be slaughtered. Sins multiplied: adultery, lying, deceit, and now murder. As judgment on David, the child resulting from adultery was born sickly and later died.

Just as Uncle Manny's poop affected his brothers, his kids, and his potential house-buyer, so did David's sins affect Bathsheba, Uriah, and finally his baby son. In David's case, his sins had very deep and grave consequences to those that "stepped" in his mess. Most importantly of all, his sins affected his relationship with the Lord God Almighty.

> *"I, the Lord your God, am a jealous God, punishing the children for the sin of the parents to the third and fourth generation of those who hate me, but showing love to a thousand generations of those who love me and keep my commandments." (Exodus 20:5-6)*

David felt the pang of punishment in losing his child as well as the guilt of his sin. Yet, he also experienced the joy of restoration with the Lord. Despite the "bad news" of sin and its inescapable consequences, there is hope in the "good news" that Christ has paid the price for our mess of sin and made us righteous and spotless in God's eyes.

Just like David, we have committed sins that have far-reaching consequences to our spouses, our children, family members, friends, or brothers and sisters in Christ. At the same time, many of us have reaped consequences of others' sins or seen its devastating effects such as unfaithfulness, divorce, betrayal or deceit. Sadly, it's easy to simply turn on the news on TV to see the evidence of the ripple effect of sin.

Just as with David, however, the good news is that we have a Savior who came for this very purpose: to help us make right of what's wrong in our lives. Yes, our messes of sin can very deeply affect people we love around us, but as we walk with the Lord, in the power of His Word, we can find redemption and forgiveness.

PRAYER

Forgiving Father, I treasure the gift You've given me. Whenever I have fallen, You have been the Hand that reached out to pick me up, brush me off, clean me up and make me better. Lord, I have sinned deeply in my life, against You and against others. I have left piles of sin around that others have stepped in. Jesus, may I always humbly recognize my propensity to sin and understand that it does not only affect me. I think of my stinky attitude that can be a trap for family members to walk into, unknowingly. Even when I throw myself a pity party and selfishly wallow in it, I must lay that at your feet, Jesus. Walk with me Lord and help me to recognize my sins as YOU see them and cleanse me so that my witness of You is pure. May my actions not cause others to stumble into big messes but instead to lead them to follow after You. Amen.

POINTS TO PONDER

Our sins can have far-reaching consequences, affecting us personally, our children, extended family members, and even strangers. It's not true that you can continue in sin and it only hurts you; sin is more like a disease that spreads, infecting those nearest to you.

1. *What kind of sinfulness have you "walked" into and how do you feel about it?*

2. *What messes have you created that becomes a mess for others as well?*

3. What emotions do you feel when your sins cause strife for others?

Scripture to Read: Exodus 20:4-6

4 "You shall not make for yourself an image in the form of anything in heaven above or on the earth beneath or in the waters below. 5 You shall not bow down to them or worship them; for I, the Lord your God, am a jealous God, punishing the children for the sin of the parents to the third and fourth generation of those who hate me, 6 but showing love to a thousand generations of those who love me and keep my commandments."

4. How many generations are punished for sin of the parents?

5. *How many generations receive blessing for loving and obeying God?*

6. *What sinful habits have been passed down from your parents, uncles, aunts, or grandparents?*

7. *What are you doing as a parent that your children watch and adopt that will affect their futures?*

8. *How can you pass down a legacy of love for God and obedience?*

9. *What does that look like practically speaking? (verse 6) Pray for one another regarding this.*

Chapter 10

Where Does Poop Go?

"The Dung Gate was repaired by Malkijah son of Rekab, ruler of the district of Beth Hakkerem. He rebuilt it and put its doors with their bolts and bars in place."
Nehemiah 3:14

In biblical times, the city of Jerusalem had several gates with different purposes: the Fish Gate, Sheep Gate, Water Gate, Fountain Gate, and the Dung Gate to name a few. Sheep and lambs used in sacrifices were bought through the Sheep Gate. The Fountain Gate was located near a local pool and would be used by Hebrews to clean before heading off to the Temple. The purpose of the Dung Gate was the avenue which to take out excrement and garbage to be burned. As you can see, the other gates had their roles and the Dung Gate's role may seem inconsequential, but without it, the city would get pretty smelly and dangerously unsanitary too.

Today, we have our own version of the Dung Gate with our modern sewage systems. Poop gets flushed down the toilet, goes through the sewer pipes underground, and eventually gets pumped to our local sewage company where *they* deal with it. The sewage is pumped in, treated, and then the water gets returned to our pipes, but as clean water. It's processed and becomes usable again.

Societies without a proper sewage system will not survive for lack of clean water. They will either have to pick up and move, leading a nomadic lifestyle, or they will perish from not having water in their current home. We see this in some third-world countries that have tribal lifestyles; organizations collect donations to help villages dig water wells so they can have clean drinking water. Otherwise, the only source of water is full of bacteria, parasites, and disease; a death sentence if consumed for entire people groups. A community will not grow in a limited place like this.

So if sin is like poop, and we have an elaborate sanitation system, where can we send our sin? Do we have "systems" in place to help us deal with sin? Some religious denominations do have times of confession where you're scheduled to see a clergyman and confess your sins. This has the benefit of accountability, but works best if you already have a relationship with your clergyman where you trust him with your secrets. Otherwise, you may limit confessions to things such as, "I hit my brother." In this method of confession, it's important to know that speaking to the clergyman doesn't take the place of confessing your sin directly to God. The clergyman is acting more as a counselor rather than the forgiver of sins, God our Father.

Other "sin sanitation" models include having an accountability or prayer partner: a brother or sister in Christ you trust with private personal baggage and who will tell you the truth in love. A great accountability partner is also dedicated to praying earnestly for you. Another person that could fit this model is a counselor or therapist – who has a bond of confidentiality, but can provide guidance and advice as well. These folks are professionally trained to help us process things, including sin, and certainly have great potential to guide us to healing. As James 5:16 urges, "Therefore, confess your sins to each other and pray for each other so that you may be healed. The prayer of a righteous man is powerful and effective."

The fact that we need healing from our sins shows that sin can make us spiritually sick and unhealthy. Poop that is not removed through our sewer systems can cause contamination of our living areas and create extreme sickness and even death. We must strive for spiritual health and wellness through regular confession and powerful prayer within our circles of faith. Just as clean poop-free living space is vital, our hearts become extremely unhealthy carrying around un-confessed sin.

Other denominations have a public time in their service for a confessional liturgy, which even names some specific sins. You can confess silently in your heart, but everyone is corporately confessing sin. It's interesting that this is similar to our sewage system; it's public, but everyone uses it privately. Growing up, my dad who is a pastor, would always pause for a silent time of confession before communion, examining our hearts as we remember Christ's sacrifice. Similarly, my prayer partner and I use a method that includes a silent time of confession right after the praise portion and before the thanksgiving portion.

Sometimes we need to confess to a fellow brother or sister that they've hurt us in some way. As difficult as it is to confront someone, it's almost like neglecting to mention they have dog poop on their shoe. They'll keep tracking it everywhere unaware of the disgusting hazard being spread. Matthew 18 instructs us to go to that person one-on-one first and then if they don't listen, bring a second person, and if they still don't listen bring the church. This involves and requires much love and prayer, as well as honesty and vulnerability. To share a hurting heart can lead to healing of the relationship if we use God's way of reconciliation properly, speaking the truth in love. If your friend or brother does not wish to reconcile then you may need to let them be. Romans 12:18 says, "If it is possible, as far as it depends on you, live at peace with everyone." Ultimately, you can only be responsible for your actions and your efforts to reconcile can only reach so far.

Since Christ's sacrifice, the veil that covered the Holy of Holies has been torn in two and now paves the way for all believers to directly approach the Lord through Christ. "Clothed…with Christ," (Galatians 3:27) we are able to approach and to confess our sins to God at any time: while driving, while cooking, while changing diapers, at home, at work, ANYWHERE! When we come to the Lord, honest about our sinfulness, He "remove[s] our transgressions from us… as far as the east is from the west," (Psalm 103:12); He "blot[s] them out of the book of the living" (Psalm 69:28); and "though your sins be as scarlet, they shall be white as snow" (Isaiah 1:18).

Forgiveness is powerful, most especially the forgiveness of the Father. You need to flush that poop down the drain! Do not delay in your time of confession, first to God, and if needed to a fellow Christian, counselor, or member of the clergy. It brings life and healing to hurting hearts.

PRAYER

Oh, Most High God, how do You do it? How do You forgive when I sinfully offend You so often? Thank You for the gift of Christ's powerful blood sacrifice. Help me to find more avenues for honest confession; whether it's to earthly brothers and sisters or to You directly. May I find a balance in both, for both are commanded in Your Word. Make me more truthful and humble in my confessions to bring about more healing of wounds and sickness in my spiritual life. To You be the glory, Lord Jesus, You have done great things. Do more great things through me. Amen.

POINTS TO PONDER

Because we are born into a world of sin and must deal daily with our personal sins, we desperately need systems to assist in cleaning up the mess of sin. Give thanks to God for providing specific instructions for us in our confession of sin.

Scripture to Read: Hebrews 9:1-10

1 Now the first covenant had regulations for worship and also an earthly sanctuary. 2 A tabernacle was set up. In its first room were the lampstand and the table with its consecrated bread; this was called the Holy Place. 3 Behind the second curtain was a room called the Most Holy Place, 4 which had the golden altar of incense and the gold-covered Ark of the Covenant. This ark contained the gold jar of manna, Aaron's staff that had budded, and the stone tablets of the covenant. 5 Above the ark were the cherubim of the Glory, overshadowing the atonement cover. But we cannot discuss these things in detail now. 6 When everything had been arranged like this, the priests entered regularly into the outer room to carry on their ministry. 7 But only the high priest entered the inner room, and that only once a year, and never without blood, which he offered for himself and for the sins the people had committed in ignorance. **8** *The Holy Spirit was showing by this that the way into the Most Holy Place had not yet been disclosed as long as the first tabernacle was still functioning.* **9** *This is an illustration for the present time, indicating that the gifts and sacrifices being offered were not able to clear the conscience of the worshiper.* **10** *They are only a matter of food and drink and various ceremonial washings—external regulations applying until the time of the new order.*

1. *How is this previous model of "sin sanitation" limiting to us as sinners needing sanctification? (See verse 7 & 9)*

2. *How does this foreshadow what's to come? (See verses 9-10)*

Scripture to Read: Hebrews 9:11-15, 24-28

11 But when Christ came as high priest of the good things that are now already here,[a] he went through the greater and more perfect tabernacle that is not made with human hands, that is to say, is not a part of this creation. **12** He did not enter by means of the blood of goats and calves; but he entered the Most Holy Place once for all by his own blood, thus obtaining[b] eternal redemption. **13** The blood of goats and bulls and the ashes of a heifer sprinkled on those who are ceremonially unclean sanctify them so that they are outwardly clean. **14** How much more, then, will the blood of Christ, who through the eternal Spirit offered himself unblemished to God, cleanse our consciences from acts that lead to death,[c] so that we may serve the living God! **15** For this reason Christ is the mediator of a new covenant, that those who are called may receive the promised eternal inheritance—now that he has died as a ransom to set them free from the sins committed under the first covenant. **24** For Christ did not enter a sanctuary made with human hands that was only a copy of the true one; he entered heaven itself, now to appear for us in God's presence. **25** Nor did he enter heaven to offer himself again and again, the *way the high priest enters the Most Holy Place every year with blood that is not his own.* **26** *Otherwise Christ would have had to suffer many times since the creation of the world. But he has appeared once for all at the culmination of the ages to do away with sin by the sacrifice of himself.* **27** *Just as people are destined to die once, and after that to face judgment,* **28** *so Christ was sacrificed once to take away the sins of many; and he will appear a second time, not to bear sin, but to bring salvation to those who are waiting for him.*

3. *By whose blood did Christ enter the Most Holy Place?*

4. *What does Christ's blood cleanse our consciences of?*

5. *What specifically has Christ cleansed your conscience of or are there things you wish your conscience was clear of now?*

6. *Where did Christ go to plead for us? (See verse 24)*

7. *How many times did Christ have to die for all our sins?*

Read the following from "Confession and Absolution," a Lutheran Liturgy:

__Pastor:__ Let us then confess our sins to God our Father.

__Congregation:__ Most merciful God, we confess that we are by nature sinful and unclean. We have sinned against you in thought, word, and deed by what we have done and by what we have left undone. We have not loved you with our whole heart. We have not loved our neighbors as ourselves. We justly deserve your present and eternal punishment. For the sake of your Son Jesus Christ, have mercy on us. Forgive us, renew us and lead us so that we may delight in your will and walk in your ways to the glory of your Holy Name.

__Pastor:__ In the mercy of Almighty God, Jesus Christ was given to die for us. And for his sake, God forgives us all our sins. To those who believe in Jesus Christ, he gives the power to become the children of God and bestows on them the Holy Spirit. May the Lord who has begun this good work in us bring it to completion in the day of our Lord Jesus Christ. (John 1:12, Philippians 1:6)

8. *Read through this once more, changing "we" to "I" and "us" to "me" whenever you see it.*

Chapter 11

Poop is Alienating

"But with you there is forgiveness, so that we can, with reverence, serve you…put your hope in the Lord, for with the Lord is unfailing love and with him is full redemption." Psalm 130:4,7

I remember as a young mom when one of my sweet babies had a liquid poop, right on my husband's grandma! She was holding my "sweet child" in her lap when this accident ensued. It had seeped out of the diaper, onto my baby's clothing, and all over Grandma's lap too! She handed the soiled and smelly child back to me and we had to do an "extract-your-child-from-this-disgustingness" operation, as well as a bath. Grandma had to do her own operation for it had gotten all over her clothing too! Later, my baby was back on her lap, cooing, smiling, and exuding that awesome baby smell; Grandma was once again delighted to have my baby in her lap again.

When a baby poops, everyone wants him to go by his mommy until she can clean him up! However, once he's clean, then everyone wants him back and they can kiss, hug, and bounce him on their knees once again! When there's poop present, it completely inhibits our ability to have fellowship with one another. It's not something that can be ignored, put off, or endured; it requires swift action and removal before enjoyment of company can resume.

Imagine that you are the baby, sitting on Grandpa's knee, but Grandpa is God. You are delighting in one another's company, smiling and laughing, playing peek-a-boo. All of a sudden a distinct aroma comes from your diaper; there is a big problem. As a baby, you can't change your own diaper; you're helpless to get rid of this barrier to your fellowship with God. Therefore, God in His infinite love changes your diaper Himself, wiping away excrement, stains, and offensive smells. Finally, He washes you fully in the bathtub. You are clean.

You're helpless without His help, but you must accept this gift and be willing to allow Him to clean you in order to receive forgiveness. Otherwise, you cannot be in His presence, because the dirty diaper (sin) makes it impossible for you to be in fellowship with one another. God has a love and delight for us, His very own creations, but sin inhibits our ability to enjoy each other. He dearly wants to help us get rid of it so we can delight in being together. We have a picture of this fellowship on earth, for we can fellowship with Him in prayer, in His Word, and with His Church. Greater still is the fellowship that those who have accepted this gift will receive in Heaven, face-to-face with the Lord. *1 Corinthians 2:9 says, "...no eye has seen...no ear has heard, and... no human mind has conceived— the things God has prepared for those who love Him."*

This cleansing is an illustration of God's forgiveness; God is the one we have offended first of all with our sins. David says to the Lord: "Against you, you only, have I sinned" (Psalm 54:1). The only agent powerful enough to cleanse such an inexcusable offense is the precious blood of Jesus Christ. His physical death and the blood that poured through his veins cleanses us and rids us of sin. Not only the sins of one sinner, but the sins of the entire world: "He is the atoning sacrifice for our sins, and not only for ours but also for the sins of the whole world" (1 John 2:2). Now that's POWER!

Sin, like poop, is not only nasty, repulsive, and dirty, but leads to death. To cover over this repulsiveness requires an extremely expensive commodity: the blood of God's one and only

Son. As the old hymn by William Cowpers says, "There is a fountain filled with blood drawn from Emmanuel's veins, and sinners plunged beneath that flood lose all their guilty stains." A fountain full of blood sounds like something out of the latest horror movie, but this vivid picture demonstrates the extremely high cost of covering our sins. Jesus' blood cannot even have an earthly price, He is the Son of God, so precious and beloved.

In the Old Testament, the requirement for forgiveness of sin was an innocent, spotless lamb, goat, or calf whose blood would be sprinkled on the Mercy Seat of the Ark of the Covenant. This was the place God met to commune with man and regularly necessitated the blood of an innocent, which atoned for sinful man. This was the only way a perfect God, devoid of sin, could possibly come in contact with man, full of sin. The amazing thing about Christ is that His sacrifice is a one-time only deal: Hebrews 9:28 states that: "Christ was sacrificed once to take away the sins of many; and he will appear a second time, not to bear sin, but to bring salvation to those who are waiting for him."

Looking at my own sins and shortcomings, I am blown away by the depth of His forgiveness and love. That the Father would forsake His only Son, to regain fellowship with me, a dirty sinner, much like a baby in a dirty diaper. Imagine if we left baby in his smelly and poopy diaper. The poor baby would be just hopeless and hurting, not knowing what to do. He would be out of fellowship with loved ones and continue in poop, unable to help himself whatsoever.

Even though we don't mean to, we cannot rationalize, excuse, or deny the guilt of our sins. Just like the little baby, we can't help it, but we're still guilty of it. Maybe you've never confessed Jesus as Lord and you want to know the power of his forgiveness: ask Him! Perhaps you are a believer and have fallen away, but want to rekindle the relationship with the Lord again: go to Him! Forgiveness is your only hope and is available to you right now, even. Forgiveness is like a clean baby's bottom; it makes the way for us to enter into fellowship with God the Father, God the Son, and God the Holy Spirit, now and for eternity.

PRAYER

Merciful Lord Jesus, You not only provided the means for me to avoid hell, my true punishment for sin, You WERE the means. As You suffered cruel torture and expired on an execution instrument shaped like a cross, Your perfect blood spilled out for me, a dirty sinner. As You rose to life eternal, You conquered death and You give me hope of eternal life as well! I praise You for the hope offered to me, a blessed gift, I'll never earn. Forgiven, forgiven, forgiven. May I walk worthy of this promise of hope, not ever forgetting the price You paid for it. Amen.

POINTS TO PONDER

Just as a wee one in a soiled diaper remains helpless to clean himself, so are we sinners unable to separate ourselves from our mess without the powerful grace of God and Christ's amazing sacrifice. Forgiveness brings us into fellowship with Almighty God. Now that's power!

Scripture to Read: Luke 7:36-50 (NIV)

***36** When one of the Pharisees invited Jesus to have dinner with him, he went to the Pharisee's house and reclined at the table. **37** A woman in that town who lived a sinful life learned that Jesus was eating at the Pharisee's house, so she came there with an alabaster jar of perfume.*

***38** As she stood behind him at his feet weeping, she began to wet his feet with her tears. Then she wiped them with her hair, kissed them and poured perfume on them. **39** When the Pharisee who had invited him saw this, he said to himself, "If this man were a prophet, he would know who is touching him and what kind of woman she is—that she is a sinner." **40** Jesus answered him, "Simon, I have something to tell you." "Tell me, teacher," he said. **41** "Two people owed money to a certain moneylender. One owed him five hundred denarii,[a] and the other fifty. **42** Neither of them had the money to pay him back, so he forgave the debts of both. Now which of them will love him more?" **43** Simon replied, "I suppose the one who had the bigger debt forgiven." "You have judged correctly," Jesus said. **44** Then he turned toward the woman and said to Simon, "Do you see this woman? I came into your house. You did not give me any water for my feet, but she wet my feet with her tears and wiped them with her hair. **45** You did not give me a kiss, but this woman, from the time I entered, has not stopped kissing my feet. **46** You did not put oil on my head, but she has poured perfume on my feet. **47** Therefore, I tell you, her many sins have been forgiven—as her great love has shown. But whoever has been* *forgiven little loves little." **48** Then Jesus said to her, "Your sins are forgiven." **49** The other guests began to say among themselves, "Who is this who even forgives sins?" **50** Jesus said to the woman, "Your faith has saved you; go in peace."*

1. Taking verses 41-43 into consideration, to whom is forgiveness available to, the one with big or small debts?

2. What is Jesus' point in telling this short parable?

3. Did this woman's reputation precede her? Cite verses to support.

4. *Was it the perfume and honor she gave Jesus that saved her or something else? Cite verses.*

5. *Why could Christ allow her to get near him and touch him?*

6. *Can you relate to this woman's story in any way?*

7. *How do you react to Christ personally when he says to you, "your sins are forgiven?" (verse 48)*

8. *What ways can you praise and thank Him for the abounding gift of forgiveness that renews fellowship with Him?*

Chapter 12

Poop Removal

"'No,' said Peter, you shall never wash my feet. Jesus answered, 'Unless I wash you, you have no part with me.'" John 13:8

A few years ago, I attended a spa-themed retreat for a ladies' chapel group that I am a part of. We had wonderful activities planned such as pairing up and massaging lotion onto our partner's hand while engaging in "girl talk." One activity involved having a peaceful prayer experience in a beautifully-prepared room including a lovely fountain and lit candles. One of the most memorable activities was a time in our large group where we were to wash one another's feet. Up until that point, everyone seemed OK with the activities, but this one was different. This activity put us on the defense. Someone was going to touch my stinky feet and wash them with water and dry them with a towel? I felt uncomfortable with this, slightly embarrassed, vulnerable, and very humbled. As my friend poured water over my feet and wiped them with the towel, a mixture of the feeling of guilt and honor crept in: guilt because she should NOT be washing my nasty feet; honor because she took the role of the servant and elevated me to a position that I did not deserve.

If someone washing my feet freaks me out, I cannot imagine how one day it will feel to need someone to change my poopy diapers if it comes down to it. Washing feet is a personal moment, but washing rear ends and private areas is even more humbling. And yet, I must remember that as a helpless baby, my mother and father, dutifully changed every single dirty diaper that I made. Think of all the adult caregivers that daily humble themselves and so lovingly serve their parent, relative, or patient by changing dirty diapers. It is their loving service to them. However, this must be difficult to exchange roles as many times the parent has to become like a child and allow their own children or nurses to care for them in this extremely intimate way.

In Biblical times, the Israelites as well as all other Orientals, wore sandals, so dust, mud, and even animal waste would get on their feet. Naturally, it was necessary to wash feet more often. It was a sign of hospitality for the host to offer water for foot washing upon a guest's arrival from a long journey; if he was wealthier, a slave would do this chore. This was considered the lowliest of tasks to do. Yet we see Jesus, on the last night of his life taking on this role of lowly servant as He stoops down to wash all twelve disciples' feet. Prior to this moment, the disciples had "an argument.... as to which of them would be the greatest" (Luke 9:46). Christ dispels this argument with His act of humility and service. According to James Orr in the *International Standard Bible Encyclopedia*, "his act of humility actually cleansed their hearts of selfish ambition, killed their pride, and taught them the lesson of love." Jesus demonstrates to the disciples that true greatness is in acts of humility and service.

It's interesting that such a simple task can cause such a mix of emotions. I imagine that Peter felt as I did when Jesus says He must wash him and Peter responds that He will never wash his feet. No, Lord, I am completely unworthy of You bending low and washing my terribly dirty feet. Jesus is wise beyond Peter's and my squirming and says, "Unless I wash you, you have no part with me" (John 13:8). We must be washed, prepared, and sinless, to be a part of Christ's kingdom in Heaven. We have to allow it, because we will be marred by sin otherwise. Have you allowed him to wash you from your sins?

PRAYER

Beautiful Savior, how humbly you kneel at MY feet, urging me to allow YOU, the Prince of Peace, the King of Kings, to wash me. I am speechless and humbled and honored to a position that I do not deserve. Yet I thank you and give you the glory for becoming a Servant-King that comes to wash away the stains of this dusty, dirty world from my tired feet. Thank you for taking away these ungodly motivations to be the greatest, the best, or the brightest and help me to follow Your example of humility in which I serve others humbly. This is true greatness in Your kingdom. May I seek that as my heart's passion and life's work. Amen.

POINTS TO PONDER

If you have already asked Christ to wash your heart of its sin, you understand the humbling feeling of our Lord willingly serving you in this way that only He can do. As we look deeper into this selfless and intimate act, meditate on the sweetness of this symbol.

1. *Have you ever been a part of a foot-washing activity or ceremony and if so, how does it make you feel to be either the foot-washer or the receiver of the washing? Imagine how it might make you feel if you haven't been to one.*

Scripture to Read: John 13:1-10

__1__ It was just before the Passover Festival. Jesus knew that the hour had come for him to leave this world and go to the Father. Having loved his own who were in the world, he loved them to the end. __2__ The evening meal was in progress, and the devil had already prompted Judas, the son of Simon Iscariot, to betray Jesus. __3__ Jesus knew that the Father had put all things under *his power, and that he had come from God and was returning to God; **4** so he got up from the meal, took off his outer clothing, and wrapped a towel around his waist. **5** After that, he poured water into a basin and began to wash his disciples' feet, drying them with the towel that was wrapped around him. **6** He came to Simon Peter, who said to him, "Lord, are you going to wash my feet?" **7** Jesus replied, "You do not realize now what I am doing, but later you will understand." **8** "No," said Peter, "you shall never wash my feet." Jesus answered, "Unless I wash you, you have no part with me." **9** "Then, Lord," Simon Peter replied, "not just my feet but my hands and my head as well!" **10** Jesus answered, "Those who have had a bath need only to wash their feet; their whole body is clean. And you are clean, though not every one of you." **11** For he knew who was going to betray him, and that was why he said not every one was clean.*

2. *According to verses 4-5, what does Jesus do with his outer clothing and what replaces it?*

3. *The towel had become his only piece of clothing, how does this deepen the significance of this already lowly task? (verse 5)*

4. *Why does Simon Peter refuse to allow him to wash his feet? Put yourself in Simon Peter's position—would you want Jesus washing your feet, why or why not?*

5. *Why is it necessary for him to allow Jesus to wash his feet? (verse 8)*

6. *According to verses 9–10, why is it not necessary for a head-to-toe bath (a parallel to baptism), but just the feet?*

Scripture to Read: John 13: 12-17

12 When he had finished washing their feet, he put on his clothes and returned to his place. "Do you understand what I have done for you?" he asked them. 13 "You call me 'Teacher' and 'Lord,' and rightly so, for that is what I am. 14 Now that I, your Lord and Teacher, have washed your feet, you also should wash one another's feet. 15 I have set you an example that you should do as I have done for you. 16 Very truly I tell you, no servant is greater than his master, nor is a messenger greater than the one who sent him. 17 Now that you know these things, you will be blessed if you do them.

7. *How is Christ's symbol of foot-washing another method we can use to confess our sins to one another? (verse 14-15)*

8. *Some denominations have foot-washing before a feast and practice this twice a year. How would a family foot-washing time or a church event like this bring people closer together?*

9. *Keep this tool in your pocket when you may be in need of confessing to someone or see a brother or sister in need of confessing. Pray about how you might humbly assist them in confessing and cleansing their heart with the foot-washing model in mind as a symbolic humble stance to take for your brother or sister. It may be you that needs the assistance with confession.*

10. *Pray for the Lord to give you the humility necessary to accept help with sin confession and purging as well as the servant-heart to help another bring their burdens to Christ.*

Epilogue

I hope you've enjoyed this unorthodox devotional and may be you've learned some deep things about yourself, Jesus, and your sin. I hope you've laughed and learned. Mostly I hope you delved into God's word and came up with new morsels of truth regarding our sin. Our great God has done wonderful works to demolish it and take it far away from us.

If you've enjoyed this, please go to www.facebook.com/sinislikepoop and share your experience and join the conversation!

www.ingramcontent.com/pod-product-compliance
Lightning Source LLC
Chambersburg PA
CBHW071524080526
44588CB00011B/1550